Copyright notice: © 2025 by Joshua Halls

Rights statement: "All rights reserved. No part of this publication may be reproduced, distributed, or transmitted in any form or by any means, including photocopying, recording, or other electronic or mechanical methods, without the prior written permission of the publisher, except in the case of brief quotations embodied in critical reviews and certain other noncommercial uses permitted by copyright law."

THE HOLY BIBLE, NEW INTERNATIONAL VERSION®, NIV® Copyright © 1973, 1978, 1984, 2011 by Biblica, Inc.® Used by permission. All rights reserved worldwide.

Cover Design: Joshua Halls

Print ISBN: 978-0-646-71722-7

Published and distributed by Joshua Halls & Australian Worship Network
info@australianworshipnetwork.com.au

AUSTRALIAN **WORSHIP NETWORK**

How to Use This Book

Worship Connect – Team Talk was written for worship teams who are hungry to go deeper — not just musically, but spiritually, relationally, and personally.

Inside you'll find powerful devotions designed to spark conversation, stir hearts, and strengthen unity. Each entry includes a focused scripture, a devotional, discussion questions, and a personal activation. These are not surface-level thoughts — they are crafted to challenge, inspire, and draw you into honest reflection and spiritual depth.

You can use this resource in a variety of ways: as part of a team devotional before rehearsal, a regular book club study, or for individual growth and reflection. Don't feel pressured to rush through it — take your time. Sit with each devotion. Share honestly. Pray deeply. Let the Holy Spirit speak through the questions and guide your application.

This book is more than a reading plan. It's a tool for transformation — for shaping not just what you do in worship, but who you are as worshippers.

I pray that through these devotions and activations you are stirred and encouraged.

INDEX

How to Use This Book	05
1. What Is Worship	06
2. Worship as a Lifestyle	08
3. Worship In Spirit and In Truth	10
4. The Heart That God Desires	12
5. Obedience As Worship	14
6. Intimacy As Worship	16
7. The Role of The Holy Spirit	18
8. Excellence In Worship	20
9. The Power of Unity	22
10. Breaking the Fear of Man	24
11. Worship as a Weapon	26
12. The Prophetic in Worship	28
13. Rest and Renewal for the Worshipper	30
14. Character Over Talent	32
15. Led by The Spirit	34
16. Creativity That Reflects the Creator	36
17. Persevering the Call	38
18. Anointed to Lead	40

INDEX

19.	Impacting Generations	42
20	The Cost of the Call	44
21	A Life of Gratitude	46
22	Boldness by the Spirit	48
23.	Carrying God's Heart	50
24.	Discerning the Moment	52
25.	When Worship Feels Empty	54
26.	Leading off the Stage	56
27.	When the Plan Changes	58
28.	Leading with Vulnerability	60
29.	Worship as Surrender	62
30.	The Spiritual Discipline of Rehearsal	64
31.	Partnering with Prophetic Words	66
32.	Hosting the Presence of God	68
33.	Worship Without Barriers	70
34.	Gifts in Community	72
35.	Understanding Our Authority	74
36.	Your Testimony	76
37.	The Song for the Next Season	78

1

What is Worship

John 4:23 (NIV) – "Yet a time is coming and has now come when the true worshipers will worship the Father in the Spirit and in truth, for they are the kind of worshipers the Father seeks."

Worship is not a song.

It's not limited to Sunday services, platforms, or instruments. Worship is a life fully surrendered to God. It is deeply personal and undeniably practical — not just a spiritual expression but a way of living. True worship is revealed in how we live, think, serve, and respond to the mercy we've received from the Lord.

John 4:23 reminds us that worship isn't tied to a location, a genre, or a style — it's tied to a posture of the heart. God is seeking worshippers who engage with Him in spirit and in truth — with authenticity and alignment to His Word. This means our worship must go beyond emotional expression or outward form. It begins in the secret place, in our daily decisions, and in consistent obedience.

As worshippers and musicians, it's easy to measure our worship by how it feels or how people respond. But God measures it by the depth of our surrender. He's looking for people who will give Him their full "yes"

— not just in moments of music, but in everyday choices, relationships, time, and talents. Every part of our lives becomes worship when it's offered to Him in faith.

Your practice session can be worship. Your humility in team conversations can be worship. Even how you handle conflict, honor others, rest well, and serve behind the scenes reveals the kind of worshipper you are.

Worship is more than a moment — it's a mindset. It's more than music — it's a move of your heart toward God in everything. Let today be a fresh invitation to see your entire life as an altar — a place where love, devotion, and surrender rise as a fragrant offering to Him.

Discussion Questions:
- What does worship in your day to day life look like?
- In what areas of your life is it hardest to live worshipfully?
- What does it look like to worship in both spirit and truth?

Takeaway Activity:

Write a "Worship Audit" journal entry. Divide a page into four areas: Time, Talent, Thought Life, and Relationships. Under each, honestly reflect: Am I offering this area to God as worship? Highlight one area where you want to surrender more fully. Spend 15 minutes in prayer, dedicating that area to God.

2

Worship as a Lifestyle

1 Corinthians 10:31 (NIV) – "So whether you eat or drink or whatever you do, do it all for the glory of God."

Worship isn't a weekly event. It's a daily decision.

Many believers unknowingly separate "worship" from everyday life — thinking it only happens during songs or services. But Scripture paints a broader picture. Colossians 3:17 teaches that whatever we do — even ordinary acts like speaking or working — can become worship when done in Jesus' name, with gratitude and reverence.

This expands the meaning of worship. It means cooking dinner, driving to work, leading your family, showing kindness, and yes — playing music — can all glorify God. It's not about performance; it's about posture. Not about perfection; but intention.

Living a lifestyle of worship means consistently inviting God into daily routines. It's honoring Him when no one's watching. It's saying "yes" to His voice, even when it costs. It's walking in holiness, humility, and gratitude — on and off the stage.

Musicians and creatives often see worship through the lens of expression. But expression without obedience isn't worship — it's performance. True worship is rooted in relationship, and relationships thrive through consistent connection. A worship lifestyle grows through prayer, the Word, and ongoing surrender.

Ask yourself: is my private life aligned with what I express publicly? Do I treat others with the grace I sing about? Do I honour God with my habits and attitudes?

You don't need a microphone to worship — just a surrendered heart. When worship becomes your lifestyle, your music carries weight, your leadership bears fruit, and your life becomes a constant offering to God.

Discussion Questions:
- In what ways do you compartmentalise worship instead of living it out daily?
- How do you respond when your private life doesn't reflect what you express in worship?
- What's one thing you could shift this week to align more with a worship lifestyle?

Takeaway Activity:

Create a "Worship Lifestyle Map." On a blank page, list your typical day or week (morning routines, work, meals, relationships, creative time). Beside each, write how that moment could become an act of worship. Post it somewhere visible as a daily reminder to invite God into everything you do.

3

Worship in Spirit and in Truth

John 4:24 (NIV) – "God is spirit, and his worshipers must worship in the Spirit and in truth."

When Jesus met the Samaritan woman at the well, He shattered her expectations of worship. She focused on where worship happened — which mountain, which tradition. But Jesus shifted the conversation to how and who we worship. He said true worshippers must worship the Father in Spirit and in truth.

To worship in Spirit means being led by the Holy Spirit — not bound by rituals or routines, but alive to God's presence. It flows from the inside out, not the outside in. Spirit-led worship goes beyond music; it's birthed in deep communion with God — vibrant, heartfelt, and personal.

To worship in truth means our worship must be rooted in God's Word and aligned with who He is. It's not about stirring emotion or chasing trends — it's about reflecting His character, commands, and covenant. Truth gives worship substance over style.

Spirit and truth together form the foundation of authentic worship. Spirit without truth can drift into emotionalism; truth without Spirit can become dry or performative. But when they work in harmony, worship becomes a powerful encounter that transforms lives and glorifies God.

As worshippers and musicians, we must pursue both. Are we tuned to the Spirit's leading, even if it takes us off-script? Are we anchored in Scripture, so our lyrics, choices, and values reflect Him accurately?

God isn't looking for perfect performances — He's seeking worshippers. The way we live, love, and respond to Him matters more than our setlist. True worship must be spiritually alive and biblically grounded.

Let's not go through the motions. Let's worship with deep passion and unwavering truth.

Discussion Questions:
- What does it mean to you personally to worship in "Spirit"?
- How do you stay grounded in truth as a worshipper?
- Have you ever leaned too heavily on emotion or too heavily on structure in worship? What was the result?
- How can you grow in balancing Spirit and truth in your personal worship life?

Takeaway Activity:

Set aside 30 minutes this week for "Spirit and Truth" worship time. First, read a Psalm out loud (e.g., Psalm 103). Then invite the Holy Spirit to speak to your heart as you worship freely (with or without music). Write down anything God shows you during this time — thoughts, impressions, or Scripture.

4

The Heart that God Desires

1 Samuel 16:7 (NIV) – "The Lord does not look at the things people look at. People look at the outward appearance, but the Lord looks at the heart."

God is not impressed by our platforms, our production, or our performance.

What captures His attention is the posture of our heart. When the prophet Samuel was sent to anoint Israel's next king, he assumed it would be the strongest, most impressive son. But God made it clear: He doesn't look at what people see. He looks at the heart. God was seeking someone after His own heart — not after status, skill, or charisma.

This truth speaks directly to worshippers and musicians today. It's easy to focus on the external: how we sound, how we present, how people respond. But God isn't drawn to the show — He's drawn to sincerity. He's looking for purity, humility, and authenticity. Our culture values production — but God values presence.

Psalm 24 reminds us that to stand in the presence of God, we must have clean hands and a pure heart. That doesn't mean being flawless — but it does mean being surrendered. A pure heart is honest before God. It doesn't hide behind performance or image. It brings everything — the good, the broken, the real — and lays it at His feet.

God is seeking worshippers more concerned with holiness than visibility. He values brokenness over brilliance. He welcomes honesty over hype. What He desires most is a heart fully His.

So examine your heart. Is your worship about connecting with God or gaining approval? Are you guarding your heart from pride, comparison, or bitterness? God can do extraordinary things through a life surrendered to Him.

Let your heart lead your hands. Let your relationship with God shape the sound you release. When your heart is right with Him, your worship carries eternal weight — not because of how it sounds, but because of who it glorifies.

Discussion Questions:
- How do you maintain a pure heart in your worship journey?
- What outward things tend to distract you from inward devotion?
- How do you respond when God exposes heart issues?
- What qualities do you think God is really looking for in a worshipper?

Takeaway Activity:

Spend 15 minutes in quiet reflection. Ask God to search your heart (Psalm 139:23–24). Write down anything He highlights — areas needing repentance, healing, or deeper surrender. Finish by reading Psalm 51 as a prayer.

5

Obedience as Worship

1 Samuel 15:22 (NIV) – "To obey is better than sacrifice, and to heed is better than the fat of rams."

Worship isn't just about singing — it's also about obeying.

In 1 Samuel 15, King Saul offered sacrifices to God but ignored His clear command. On the surface, it looked like worship. But God rejected Saul's offering — not because the sacrifice itself was wrong, but because his heart was disobedient. The prophet Samuel delivered a sobering truth: to obey is better than sacrifice. God cares more about the posture of our hearts than the performance of our hands.

This truth remains just as relevant today. We may bring beautiful songs, powerful moments, and moving expressions of worship — but if our lives are not marked by obedience, it's just noise. True worship isn't measured by sound or stage presence, but by surrender. Obedience is worship in its purest form. It says, "God, You are worthy of my trust, even when I don't understand. I'll follow You, even when it's hard."

Genuine worship means submitting to God's voice, not just celebrating His presence. Jesus made it plain: "If you love me, keep my commands." Love without obedience is just lip service. But when we obey Him — in purity, in our relationships, in how we serve, in everyday faith — our whole life becomes a living love song to the Lord.

As worshippers and leaders, we carry spiritual influence. Our example speaks loudly. Obedience protects the purity and power of our worship. It brings integrity to our expression and alignment with the One we proclaim. In a world full of noise, let your obedience be the loudest sound in the room.

Because in the end, it's not just the songs we sing that move heaven — it's the lives we live in response to His voice.

Discussion Questions:
- What does it look like to worship God with your obedience?
- Have you ever offered something to God while ignoring His instruction?
- Why do you think obedience is so important to God?
- What is one area where God is calling you to take a step of obedience right now?

Takeaway Activity:

Write a letter to God expressing your willingness to obey, even when it's difficult. Identify one area in your life where you sense God nudging you to obey Him more fully. Take a small action step this week as a response.

6

Intimacy with God

James 4:8 (NIV) – "Come near to God and he will come near to you."

Intimacy is at the core of true worship.
It's not about performance — it's about proximity. Worship was never meant to be a distant ritual; it was always about personal connection. God has never been interested in distant devotion. His heart has always longed for closeness with His people. James 4:8 offers a profound promise: If you draw near to God, He will draw near to you. That nearness isn't reserved for the spiritually elite — it's available to anyone who pursues Him.

God desires deep, personal relationship more than polished performance. David, a worshipper after God's own heart, had one consuming desire — not for success, fame, or even blessing — but to dwell in God's presence and gaze on His beauty. That longing shaped his life and fueled his worship. It was the source of both his strength and his songs.

As worshippers and musicians, it's easy to get caught in the momentum of ministry — always preparing, leading, producing. But in all the doing, we must not forget to simply be with God. Intimacy cannot be rushed. It is cultivated through stillness, pursuit, and vulnerability. It's in that secret place where your songs are born, your soul is strengthened, and your spirit is renewed.

When we prioritize intimacy with God, everything else flows from that place — creativity, clarity, authority, and endurance. Our worship becomes more than an offering; it becomes a reflection of genuine relationship and deep friendship with Him.

What God wants most is you. Not just your gift. Not just your ability. He wants your heart — fully surrendered and fully present. He wants to meet with you, not just on stage, but in your room, your journal, your prayer walks.

Make space for Him — and watch how He meets you there.

Discussion Questions:
- How would you describe your current intimacy with God?
- What does intimacy with God look like practically in your daily life?
- What distractions or habits tend to steal time from His presence?
- How can intimacy shape your expression of worship?

Takeaway Activity:

Schedule a 1-hour personal "worship retreat" this week. Turn off distractions, prepare a quiet space, and spend time in worship, Scripture, and prayer. Don't rush. Ask God to reveal more of Himself to you — and journal what you experience.

7

The Role of the Holy Spirit

Romans 8:14 (NIV) – "For those who are led by the Spirit of God are the children of God."

The Holy Spirit is not a background figure in worship — He is the breath that brings worship to life.

He's not a silent observer or passive presence. He is the living power of God who activates our praise and draws us into deeper connection with the Father. Every true worshipper must learn to walk in step with the Spirit. Romans 8:14 says those led by the Spirit are the children of God — not as an extra, but as part of our identity and calling.

The Holy Spirit is our guide, comforter, teacher, and helper. He doesn't just inspire — He empowers. He reveals what pleases the Father and helps us walk it out. Without the Spirit, worship is just performance. With Him, it becomes encounter — alive, powerful, and transformative.

In John 14:26, Jesus promised the Spirit would teach us all things and remind us of what He said — including how we worship. He leads us in song choices, spontaneous moments, and heart posture. He may stir a prophetic lyric, direct a pause, or guide us into deeper surrender — always pointing to Jesus.

We need the Spirit to breathe on what we offer. He brings life to our preparation and freshness to familiar melodies. He softens hearts, opens ears, and awakens faith. With Him, worship becomes a supernatural bridge between heaven and earth.

Don't treat the Spirit like an add-on or emotional bonus. Invite Him into everything — rehearsal, worship sets, leadership, and personal devotion. He doesn't just inspire moments — He shapes movements.

The Holy Spirit is not a guest in worship — He is the host. And when we follow His lead, lives are changed.

Discussion Questions:
- What does it mean to you to be "led by the Spirit" in worship?
- How often do you intentionally invite the Holy Spirit into your creative or worship process?
- Can you think of a time when the Holy Spirit shifted something in worship? What happened?
- How can you grow in sensitivity to the Holy Spirit's leading?

Takeaway Activity:

Before your next worship time (personal or team), take 10 minutes to sit silently and ask the Holy Spirit to lead you. Write down anything you sense — impressions, Scriptures, words, or pictures — and lean into that during your worship.

8

Excellence in Worship

Colossians 3:23–24 (NIV) – "Whatever you do, work at it with all your heart, as working for the Lord, not for human masters."

Excellence in worship isn't about perfection — it's about devotion.

God deserves our best. Whether we're leading a congregation or practicing in private, the way we approach our craft reflects our honour for Him. Excellence isn't driven by ego or comparison — it's fueled by love for the One we serve and a desire to reflect His worth through what we bring.

Colossians 3 reminds us that whatever we do should be done "with all our heart, as working for the Lord." That includes every part of worship — our musicianship, planning, leadership, and preparation. Psalm 33 encourages us to play skillfully before the Lord — not out of pressure, but as a joyful, reverent response to His greatness. Pursuing excellence is not a burden — it's an act of worship.

Excellence is about intention. It's showing up on time, being spiritually prepared, learning your parts, and receiving feedback. It's caring about the details without being controlled by them. It's stewarding your gifts, not showcasing them. It's aligning your effort with God's heart, not chasing perfection to impress others.

God doesn't require flawlessness — He values faithfulness. But that doesn't mean we settle. It means we keep growing. We don't use "authenticity" as an excuse for lack of preparation. We grow because He is worthy.

Excellence with a pure heart draws people in. It clears the way for encounter. Done with humility and love, it reflects God's beauty, order, and majesty.

So grow in your skill. Refine your craft. Not to impress, but to honour. Let your excellence point to the excellence of the One you worship.

Discussion Questions:
- How do you define "excellence" in worship?
- What's the difference between excellence and performance?
- Are there areas where you've become lazy or casual in your preparation?
- How can you grow in skill and heart this season?

Takeaway Activity:

Set a goal to develop one specific skill (vocal, instrumental, leadership, songwriting). Create a plan with weekly steps, and dedicate each practice session as an offering to God.

9

The Power of Unity

Psalm 133:1 (NIV) – "How good and pleasant it is when God's people live together in unity!"

Unity is not just a nice idea — it's a spiritual force.

Psalm 133 doesn't just say unity is "good and pleasant"— it declares that unity is where God commands His blessing. That's not just poetic — it's powerful. When a worship team walks in unity, it creates an atmosphere where the Holy Spirit is welcomed, pride loses its grip, and hearts become soft and open. Unity paves the way for God's presence to move freely.

In John 17, one of Jesus' final prayers before the cross was for His followers to be one — just as He and the Father are one. Why? Because unity reflects heaven. It's a witness to the world that Jesus is alive. When worship teams lead in harmony instead of competition, they reflect the heart of the Trinity — unique in role, yet united in love.

Unity doesn't mean sameness. It means a shared heart, purpose, and culture of honor. It looks like valuing each person's gift, making room for different strengths, and choosing love over ego. It means staying committed when things get messy, and laying down pride to lift others up.

The enemy knows the power of unity, which is why worship teams are often attacked with offense, insecurity, and division. When unity breaks, the authority of our worship weakens. That's why we're called to guard our hearts and protect connection at all costs.

Fight for unity. Be quick to forgive, eager to encourage, and intentional about building trust. Celebrate others' wins and stay rooted in love. When we worship as one, our sound carries weight — and heaven responds.

Because united worship is more than music — it's a move of God.

Discussion Questions:
- What does unity look like in a worship team context?
- What attitudes or behaviours can threaten team unity?
- How can you personally contribute to a culture of honour and harmony?
- What do you do when offense or tension arises in the team?

Takeaway Activity:

Write a note of encouragement to someone on your team, affirming their value and unique contribution. This week, look for ways to build bridges and celebrate others.

10

Breaking the Fear of Man

Galatians 1:10 (NIV) – "Am I now trying to win the approval of human beings, or of God?"

Fear of man is one of the greatest threats to authentic worship. When we lead, create, or minister with our eyes constantly on how people are responding, we start to lose sight of why we're doing it in the first place. The desire for approval is subtle, but dangerous. Proverbs 29:25 warns us that the fear of man is a snare — a trap that can quietly entangle our motives, limit our obedience, and distort our expression of worship.

You can feel the difference: one moment you're flowing freely, and the next you're self-conscious, adjusting your choices based on who's watching, who's reacting, or who might be judging. That's not worship — that's performance. And while excellence matters, approval addiction is bondage. When we rely on applause or affirmation to feel secure in our calling, we've exchanged intimacy with God for validation from people.

True worship requires freedom. Freedom from needing to be liked. Freedom from the fear of failure. Freedom to follow the Holy Spirit even if it stretches us, challenges norms, or leads into the unknown. Galatians 1:10 makes it clear — we can't serve two masters. We have to decide: will we live to please people, or to please God?

This doesn't mean we stop valuing feedback, unity, or spiritual leadership. But it does mean we anchor our identity in God's voice, not the crowd's response. We must build our confidence in His calling, not their clapping.

Break free from performance-driven worship. Let go of the pressure to impress. Lead, sing, play, and create for an audience of One — the only One who sees the heart. Because the more your fear of man decreases, the more your freedom in worship will increase. And where there is freedom, there is power.

Discussion Questions:

- How does fear of people affect your worship leading or creativity?
- What are some signs that fear of man may be influencing your decisions?
- How can we cultivate boldness and security in God's approval?
- Have you ever had a breakthrough moment of freedom in worship?

Takeaway Activity:

Spend time declaring God's truth over yourself (Psalm 27:1, 2 Tim 1:7, Isa 41:10). Then write a "freedom statement" — one sentence that declares your intention to worship boldly, free from fear.

11

Worship as a Weapon

2 Chronicles 20:21–22 (NIV) – "As they began to sing and praise, the Lord set ambushes against the men... and they were defeated."

It's more than emotion. More than melody. It's a spiritual act of war. In 2 Chronicles 20, when King Jehoshaphat faced a vast army, he didn't send out warriors first — he sent out worshippers. Singers led the way, declaring the goodness of God before a single sword was drawn. And as they worshipped, God moved. Confusion struck the enemy camp, and victory came — not through military might, but through praise. Their worship became their breakthrough.

This story reveals a powerful truth: worship is not passive — it's active. It changes the spiritual atmosphere. It silences fear and shakes darkness. When you lift your voice in the middle of fear, pain, or uncertainty, you're not denying reality — you're declaring a greater one. You're proclaiming that God is still sovereign, still present, still worthy — no matter what surrounds you. That declaration releases faith and invites heaven's power into the battle.

Psalm 149 describes praise as a two-edged sword — one side that exalts God, and one that defeats the enemy. Worship is warfare. It doesn't just impact you — it impacts the environment around you. It can bring breakthrough to your team, your church, your family, even your city. Praise unlocks what striving never could.

Don't underestimate the power of your voice. You might feel like you're "just singing," but in the Spirit, you're contending. You're building altars, breaking chains, and pushing back darkness. Your worship is a sound of resistance, of victory, of unshakable faith.

Your praise might be the very thing that leads someone else into their freedom. So sing boldly. Worship fully. Because when you lift your voice, heaven responds — and hell trembles.

Discussion Questions:
- How do you see worship as spiritual warfare?
- Can you share a time when worship helped you through a battle?
- Why do you think the enemy tries to silence our worship?
- How can your team grow in bold, faith-filled worship?

Takeaway Activity:

Identify a current challenge or spiritual battle in your life. Create a worship playlist that declares God's victory over that area. Spend time daily singing or declaring truth over it for 7 days.

12

The Prophetic in Worship

1 Corinthians 14:3 (NIV) – "But the one who prophesies speaks to people for their strengthening, encouraging and comfort."

Prophetic worship releases heaven's heart in the moment.
It steps beyond the structure of rehearsed songs and ventures into the spontaneous, Spirit-led flow. It's where worship becomes more than music — it becomes a message. Prophetic worship may look like a spontaneous melody rising from deep within, a bold declaration that shifts the atmosphere, a spoken encouragement, or a Scripture that suddenly comes alive. In these moments, it's not just music we're offering — it's God's heart being revealed in real time.

1 Corinthians 14:3 tells us that prophecy is meant to strengthen, encourage, and comfort. Prophetic worship does exactly that. It breaks through walls, softens hearts, revives dry places, and opens spiritual ears to what God is saying now. It's not simply emotional — it's transformational. It awakens the spirit and invites people to engage with heaven in a fresh, living way.

The goal is never to be mystical or strange. The goal is clarity — to hear heaven and respond with obedience. Prophetic worship isn't about drawing attention to ourselves; it's about pointing people to

Jesus with precision and power. It's not about putting on a show — it's about serving people with God's Word, sung or spoken, in the exact moment they need it most.

As you grow in intimacy with the Lord, you'll start to sense His promptings more clearly. His whispers will become familiar, and His nudges more trusted. In those moments, don't hold back. Sing the melody that wasn't planned. Speak the word that burns in your heart. Declare hope over the weary and truth over the uncertain. Prophetic worship happens when we align our sound with what heaven is already saying.

And when we do, worship doesn't just fill a room — it transforms it.

Discussion Questions:
- What is prophetic worship in your own words?
- How do you sense God speaking during worship moments?
- How can we grow in discerning what is from God vs. personal emotion?
- What boundaries help keep prophetic expressions healthy?

Takeaway Activity:
During your next worship time, ask the Holy Spirit to give you a phrase, image, or melody. Journal what you receive. If appropriate, share it with a mentor or worship leader for wisdom and encouragement.

13

Rest & Renewal for the Worshipper

Matthew 11:28–30 (NIV) – "Come to me, all you who are weary and burdened, and I will give you rest."

Even worshippers can burn out.

In a culture driven by constant output and performance, rest is often overlooked — but it's not optional. Rest isn't laziness or weakness; it's a spiritual discipline. It's how we acknowledge our limits and return to our Source. In Matthew 11, Jesus gives us an invitation: "Come to Me, all who are weary and burdened, and I will give you rest." He doesn't offer more to carry — He offers rest for our souls.

Worship ministry can be emotionally and spiritually draining. We carry burdens, show up consistently, and pour out week after week — yet often forget to refill. Over time, even the most passionate worshippers can find themselves running dry. We're not just vessels to be emptied; we're temples meant to be filled. Exodus 33 reminds us that it's in His presence we find rest — not in entertainment or escape, but in encounter.

Rest isn't inactivity — it's intentional renewal. It's making space to be restored. It's stepping away from the noise so we can return stronger, clearer, and more alive. If we don't learn to rest, our ministry will become mechanical, and our worship will lose its depth.

Even Jesus withdrew regularly to be alone with the Father — not out of weakness, but because He knew where true strength comes from. Ministry that lasts flows out of relationship, not just responsibility.

Don't wait for burnout to start seeking rest. Build it into your rhythm now. Prioritize silence, Sabbath, joy, and reflection. Worship outside the platform. Be refreshed, not just emotionally, but spiritually.

God moves through the rested worshipper. When you rest in Him, you return with strength, clarity, and fresh anointing.

Discussion Questions:
- Do you have a healthy rhythm of rest in your life?
- What drains you most in your ministry or worship role?
- How does rest connect to spiritual renewal?
- What boundaries can you set to protect your health and longevity?

Takeaway Activity:

Schedule a personal retreat day — even if it's just 3–4 hours. Turn off your phone. Bring your Bible, journal, and no agenda. Let God speak, refill, and renew you.

14

Character Over Talent

1 Samuel 16:7 (NIV) – "People look at the outward appearance, but the Lord looks at the heart."

Talent may get you noticed — but character keeps you there.

In a culture that celebrates gifting, God continues to prioritize integrity. Skill may capture attention, but it's the heart that sustains influence. Worship leaders and musicians can be incredibly gifted — vocally, creatively, musically — yet still lack the humility and maturity that ministry requires. God isn't impressed by talent; He's drawn to a surrendered heart.

When Samuel was sent to anoint Israel's next king, he assumed it would be the most impressive or qualified-looking son. But God corrected him: "Man looks at the outward appearance, but the Lord looks at the heart." David wasn't chosen because of his status or skill, but because of the condition of his heart. It's a reminder that what we cultivate in secret matters far more than how we perform in public.

Your gifts may open doors, but your character determines if you can remain effective once you walk through them. Ministry isn't just about what you bring to the platform — it's about who you are behind the scenes. Are you teachable? Do you honor others? Are you consistent in private as well as public? Do you serve without needing credit?

Proverbs says a good name is more valuable than great riches. In our context, that includes success, applause, and opportunities. Your character is your credibility. It's what builds trust, sustains momentum, and carries weight in the Kingdom.

God isn't looking for polished performances — He's looking for pure hearts. Let your life be the loudest worship song you sing. Your integrity matters. Because in the end, it's not talent that leaves a legacy — it's the heart behind it.

Discussion Questions:
- Why is character more important than talent in worship ministry?
- What areas of your character is God refining right now?
- How can we stay grounded as our gifts grow?
- What are the dangers of relying on talent alone?

Takeaway Activity:
Ask a trusted mentor or leader for honest feedback about your character. Identify one area to grow in (e.g., humility, patience, consistency) and journal your progress over the next month.

15

Led by the Spirit

Romans 8:14 (NIV) – "For those who are led by the Spirit of God are the children of God."

Worship is more than planning — it's partnering.

Worship leadership isn't just about building a great setlist or executing transitions. It's about walking with the Holy Spirit — before, during, and after every moment. Romans 8 reminds us that the children of God are led by the Spirit, not just in life's big decisions, but in daily moments — including worship. Leadership in worship is about partnership, not performance.

Galatians 5 calls us to "keep in step with the Spirit." That means being sensitive, surrendered, and willing to respond in real time. It takes more than musical ability — it takes spiritual awareness. Sometimes that means adjusting your plan on the spot. A spontaneous moment, an extended chorus, a quiet pause — these aren't distractions; they're often where heaven breaks in.

Preparation matters. We honor God when we prepare well. But we must also stay flexible. The Holy Spirit may nudge you in a new direction mid-set. You might feel prompted to wait, to sing a different song, or to speak a word of encouragement. The goal isn't to execute perfectly — it's to respond faithfully.

Leading worship isn't about following a script — it's about staying connected to what God is doing in the room. That requires discernment, humility, and boldness. Invite the Holy Spirit into your planning — but also into the moment.

When He leads, transformation follows. Stay open, stay tuned, and be ready to move when He moves.

Discussion Questions:
- How can you grow in sensitivity to the Holy Spirit during worship?
- What does "keeping in step" with the Spirit look like practically?
- Can you recall a time when the Spirit redirected your worship moment?
- How do preparation and spontaneity work together?

Takeaway Activity:

This week, spend time praying in the Spirit before each worship set. Ask God for insight, direction, or any impression He wants you to carry into the room. Write down what you sense.

16

Creativity that Reflects the Creator

Genesis 1:27 (NIV) – "So God created mankind in his own image..."

You were made in the image of the ultimate Creator.

That means creativity isn't a side skill or a nice bonus — it's woven into your very design. Creativity isn't just what you do; it's part of who you are. Every melody you compose, every lyric you labor over, every arrangement or idea you bring to the table — these are not just artistic expressions. They are sacred opportunities to reflect the beauty, truth, and majesty of the God who formed you.

In Exodus 35, we see God's Spirit empowering artisans, designers, and craftsmen to build the tabernacle — to create things that would hold His glory. Their skill wasn't just natural talent — it was anointed. That same Spirit is still at work in creatives today. From songwriting to stage design, from tech to storytelling, creativity has always had a place in the worship of God. But it's important to remember: creativity isn't confined to the arts. It's also in innovation, in fresh thinking, in the courage to see a challenge through a new lens.

You don't have to copy what's already been done. You weren't made to replicate — you were made to reveal. The Creator of galaxies lives in you, and your creativity can carry heaven's fingerprints. So take risks. Write from the raw places. Explore sounds that haven't been heard before. Let your imagination be stirred by the Spirit — not just by trends. Originality in the Kingdom isn't about being different for difference's sake, but about uncovering something eternal through the lens of the Spirit.

But never forget the why. Creativity in worship isn't for applause — it's for alignment. Its purpose isn't to impress people, but to express God's nature. The most powerful creative offerings flow from intimacy with Him, not from ego or ambition.

So stay rooted. Stay close to the Source. When creativity flows from a heart of worship, it does more than move a room — it moves heaven.

Discussion Questions:
- How do you currently use your creativity in worship?
- Do you ever struggle to see your creativity as spiritual?
- How can we keep our creative pursuits rooted in God's heart?
- What would it look like to create from intimacy, not insecurity?

Takeaway Activity:
Spend time creating something this week purely for God — a song, a journal entry, a piece of visual art, a spoken word. Don't edit it for others. Offer it as private worship to Him.

17

Persevering the Call

Galatians 6:9 (NIV) – "Let us not become weary in doing good, for at the proper time we will reap a harvest if we do not give up."

Worship ministry is not always easy — but it is always worth it.

There will be seasons where you feel poured out, overlooked, and underappreciated. Times when the passion you once had feels distant, and the work feels heavier than the joy. Fatigue creeps in. Disappointment whispers. Rejection stings. Even your own spirit may feel dry — like you're giving out more than you're receiving. But in those moments, we return to the Word. Galatians 6 reminds us: Do not grow weary in doing good, for at the proper time, you will reap a harvest — if you do not give up.

Ministry isn't about constant excitement — it's about consistent obedience. It's not measured by how inspired you feel, but by how faithful you remain. God isn't looking for polished perfection; He's looking for people who will keep showing up. Who will keep sowing when the ground looks barren. Who will keep singing even when the room feels empty. Like Paul told Timothy, the goal isn't just to start strong — it's to finish well. That's the call: Fight the good fight. Keep the faith. Finish the race.

The enemy knows the power of a persevering worshipper. He would love nothing more than to wear you down, to make you question your calling, to convince you it's not making a difference. But every note sung in obedience, every rehearsal attended in weariness, every whispered prayer behind closed doors — it all matters. Nothing is wasted in the Kingdom. What feels small to you may be planting something eternal in someone else.

So hold on. Stay rooted in truth, not in emotion. Keep pressing in. You may not see the fruit today, but the seeds you're sowing are alive. They will bloom — in your life, in your team, and in every heart that your worship touches.

Faithfulness is never wasted. Stay the course — the harvest is coming.

Discussion Questions:
- What has challenged your perseverance in ministry?
- How do you stay faithful when you feel unseen or tired?
- Why is endurance important in worship ministry?
- Who inspires you with their spiritual longevity?

Takeaway Activity:

Write a letter to your future self — the version of you who might want to quit someday. Remind yourself of your calling, your "why," and the harvest ahead. Keep it in a place you can revisit when you need strength.

18

Anointed to Lead

1 Samuel 16:13 (NIV) – "So Samuel took the horn of oil and anointed him in the presence of his brothers, and from that day on the Spirit of the Lord came powerfully upon David."

God doesn't just call you to lead — He anoints you to do it.

He doesn't throw you into leadership and leave you to figure it out on your own. From the very beginning, God equips those He appoints. David was just a young shepherd boy when the prophet Samuel anointed him — yet the Spirit of God came upon him with power from that day forward. David didn't step into the fullness of his calling immediately, but the anointing marked him, set him apart, and prepared him for the journey ahead.

That same Spirit — the same anointing that empowered David — is available to you today. Worship leadership is not about a platform, a title, or natural talent. It's about being chosen, equipped, and empowered by God's presence. The anointing is what makes the difference. It's the supernatural enablement that breathes life into your leadership. It's what breaks chains, stirs hearts, and shifts atmospheres. Without it, all we offer is noise. But with it, lives are changed and heaven touches earth.

You don't need to strive, compete, or compare. You simply need to steward what God has given you, stay faithful in the small things, and remain filled with His Spirit. The anointing isn't earned — it's carried. And it flows best through a surrendered heart.

Zechariah 4:6 reminds us: "Not by might, nor by power, but by My Spirit," says the Lord. Our efforts, no matter how polished, will never produce what only the Spirit can do. This kind of leadership flows from closeness to God. The anointing doesn't come through hustle or hype — it flows from intimacy, prayer, and a life laid down.

Stay close to Him. Guard your time in His presence. Let your leadership be rooted in relationship, not routine. Because when the anointing is present, everything changes — not just for you, but for everyone you lead.

Discussion Questions:
- What do you think it means to be anointed by God?
- How do you know when you're leading in your own strength vs. by the Spirit?
- How can you cultivate a lifestyle that stays sensitive to the anointing?
- In what ways can anointed leadership impact your team and congregation?

Takeaway Activity:

Take 30 minutes this week to pray and worship alone, asking the Holy Spirit to freshly anoint you for the role you carry. Write down what He speaks to your heart.

19

Impacting Generations

Psalm 145:4 (NIV) – "One generation commends your works to another; they tell of your mighty acts."

Your worship echoes beyond today.

It's not just a momentary expression — it's an eternal investment. Psalm 145 speaks of a generational legacy of worship: "One generation will commend your works to another; they will tell of your mighty acts." When we worship, we're not only responding to who God is — we're also planting seeds of faith in the hearts of those who come after us. Whether you're a parent, mentor, leader, or friend, your worship sets a tone. It becomes a living example that others will follow, often more than you realize.

We live in a culture obsessed with instant results — fast feedback, quick wins, and viral moments. But God moves with a generational mindset. He sees farther than we do. Your private obedience and public praise today can spark something powerful in the life of a child, a team member, or someone quietly watching. Your consistency — in the highs and the lows — builds a foundation that can outlast you. What you cultivate now will either bless or burden the generations that follow.

Worship is more than words and melodies — it's a lifestyle that leaves a mark. And it's more often caught than taught. The next generation is watching. They're listening to how you sing, yes — but more importantly, they're watching how you live. Will your life show them how to praise through pain? How to cling to truth when it's costly? How to hunger for God's presence when it's not popular?

This isn't just about being a worshipper — it's about raising them. Building a culture where worship isn't just practiced, but passed on. Where praise isn't a performance, but a pattern they can follow.

So worship boldly. Live faithfully. Leave a legacy of love for God that outlives your voice.

Discussion Questions:
- Who impacted your worship life growing up or early in your walk?
- How are you investing in the next generation of worshippers?
- Why is it important to think generationally in ministry?
- What legacy do you want to leave behind?

Takeaway Activity:

Take time this week to encourage, teach, or spend time with someone younger in the faith or in ministry. Share your story, pray with them, or invite them to serve alongside you.

20

The Cost of the Call

Luke 9:23 (NIV) – "Whoever wants to be my disciple must deny themselves and take up their cross daily and follow me."

True worship will cost you something.

We love the idea of following Jesus, but often resist the sacrifice that comes with it. Worship isn't just about songs — it's about surrender. It's about laying something down in love and devotion. In 2 Samuel 24, when King David was offered a free sacrifice, he refused. He said, "I will not offer to the Lord that which costs me nothing." That moment reveals something powerful: worship without cost isn't worship at all — it's convenience.

Jesus never sugarcoated the call to follow Him. He made it clear that true discipleship means dying to self daily. That doesn't mean we live in misery — it means we live in freedom. When you're surrendered, you're no longer chained to your ego, your comfort, or the need for applause. Surrender unlocks clarity. It deepens intimacy. The more surrendered you are, the more powerful and pure your worship becomes.

Being a true worshipper may cost you something tangible — popularity, convenience, recognition, or even relationships. But the Kingdom always trades temporary loss for eternal gain. Every unseen act of obedience, every private sacrifice, every "yes" that no one else applauds — it all matters to God. He sees it. He values it. And He uses it.

Don't underestimate the power of your private altar. God honors what's given in secret. And when you give Him everything — not just your voice, but your pride, your plans, your comfort — you'll discover a deeper kind of abundance. You may lose what doesn't matter, but you'll gain what truly does.

Let your worship be marked by sacrifice. Let it carry weight. Let it cost you something — because that's the sound heaven cannot ignore. It's not just melody — it's devotion. And when God hears that sound, He moves.

Discussion Questions:
- What has following Jesus cost you personally?
- Why is sacrifice essential to authentic worship?
- Are there areas where you've been withholding from God?
- How can you embrace the cost of your calling with joy?

Takeaway Activity:
Write a prayer of surrender, listing anything God may be calling you to lay down. Offer it as an act of worship this week.

21

A Life of Gratitude

Psalm 100:4 (NIV) – "Enter his gates with thanksgiving and his courts with praise..."

Gratitude is the doorway to worship.

It's more than a feeling — it's a posture that prepares the heart to encounter God. Worship doesn't begin with a chord or a lyric; it begins with thanksgiving. God isn't just looking for people who know how to do worship — He's looking for people who know how to live thankful. Gratitude shifts your focus. It opens your eyes to His faithfulness, even in seasons of struggle or waiting.

Thanksgiving is a powerful weapon. It pushes back entitlement, silences comparison, and breaks through despair. When life feels uncertain, gratitude anchors you to what's unshakable — the goodness and character of God. That's why Paul instructed the church to give thanks in all circumstances — not just the pleasant ones. Because gratitude doesn't depend on your current situation — it flows from who God is and what He's already done.

When we fix our eyes on His past faithfulness, faith rises for what He's yet to do. Gratitude builds expectation. It reminds us that we serve a God who has never failed — and won't start now. As worshippers, our lives should overflow with gratitude. It should be woven into our songs, our prayers, our leadership, and our conversations.

A grateful heart attracts heaven. It creates space for joy, peace, and unity to grow. Gratitude isn't blind optimism — it's clear-eyed faith in the goodness of God. Don't let what's missing rob you of the praise that's due today. There's always something to thank Him for — even breath in your lungs is a miracle.

Gratitude doesn't always change your circumstances — but it will always change you. It softens your heart, sharpens your perspective, and draws you closer to God.

Make thanksgiving your starting point — and you'll find that worship follows naturally.

Discussion Questions:
- Why do you think gratitude is essential in a worship lifestyle?
- What are signs of an ungrateful heart?
- How can gratitude shift your perspective during challenges?
- What's something you're currently taking for granted?

Takeaway Activity:

Write a gratitude list of 25 things — big or small — that you're thankful to God for. Read it aloud during your next quiet time.

22

Boldness by the Spirit

Acts 4:31 (NIV) – "They were all filled with the Holy Spirit and spoke the word of God boldly."

Worship is warfare — and it requires boldness.

Worship isn't just a peaceful moment of reflection — it's often a declaration of truth in the face of resistance. It's a spiritual act that confronts darkness, breaks chains, and releases heaven's atmosphere. When the early church was filled with the Holy Spirit, they didn't retreat in fear — they advanced in boldness. They didn't rely on personality or charisma. Their courage came from the Spirit within them. That same Spirit is available to you today.

Boldness in worship doesn't mean being loud for the sake of attention. It means being unashamed of the One you represent. It's having the courage to step forward when everything in you wants to shrink back. Whether you're leading a congregation, writing songs, praying over your team, or standing firm in a dark world, boldness is what allows you to do it with clarity, authority, and love.

As a worshipper, you carry a sound — not just in your music, but in your life — that silences fear and awakens faith. But remember: boldness isn't arrogance. It's not about pushing yourself forward — it's about elevating Christ. True boldness is rooted in love, anchored in truth, and expressed through obedience. The enemy would love nothing more than to mute your voice, to cause you to question your calling, to keep you in the shadows. But God has called you to stand tall, to speak clearly, and to live courageously.

This generation doesn't need more polished voices — it needs brave ones. We don't need performers — we need people who carry the fire of conviction. When you're filled with the Holy Spirit, fear begins to lose its grip, and boldness takes its rightful place.

You were never meant to blend in. You were called to rise up, to worship with passion, to lead with courage, and to walk in the authority of heaven.

Discussion Questions:
- What situations make you feel timid or afraid in worship?
- How can you grow in Holy Spirit boldness?
- What's the difference between boldness and pride?
- Who's someone you've seen model spiritual courage?

Takeaway Activity:

Take one action step this week that requires boldness — whether it's leading a new song, praying out loud, or sharing a testimony. Trust the Spirit to empower you.

23

Carrying God's Heart

Jeremiah 3:15 (NIV) – "Then I will give you shepherds after my own heart, who will lead you with knowledge and understanding."

More than a great voice or impressive skill, God is looking for people who carry His heart.

In worship ministry, talent may open doors — but it's the condition of your heart that determines whether you carry lasting impact. To be effective, your heart must beat in rhythm with God's — for His people, His purity, and His purpose. You're not just leading songs; you're guiding people into a holy encounter. That requires more than musical ability — it takes empathy, compassion, and spiritual discernment.

Worship leaders are called to be shepherds, not performers. Shepherds after God's own heart are marked by love, not ego. They're motivated by service, not spotlight. They don't step onto a platform to be seen — they step up to serve, with a heart that reflects the kindness and truth of Jesus. Worship isn't about how impressive you sound — it's about how deeply you care for the people God has entrusted to you.

God entrusts His presence to those He can trust with His people. Carrying His heart means loving the broken without judgment, embracing the outsider without fear, and forgiving even when it hurts. It means choosing gentleness over pride, patience over pressure, and humility over hype. It's a life shaped not by ambition, but by the cross.

When people encounter God's heart through you — through your words, your attitude, your actions — they begin to see that He is trustworthy. They may come for the music, but they stay when they feel His love. Your ability to reflect His heart may speak louder than any lyric ever could.

So don't just represent worship — represent the One you worship. Let every note, every prayer, and every conversation be marked by the heart of the Father. Because when people sense His heart in you, they'll be drawn to His hands..

Discussion Questions:
- How do you recognize when your heart is aligned with God's?
- What does it look like to carry God's heart in your worship ministry?
- How can love shape the way you lead others?
- Where in your life do you need more compassion?

Takeaway Activity:

Spend time in prayer asking God to give you His heart for someone you find hard to love. Write their name down and look for a way to serve or bless them this week.

24

Discerning the Moment

Romans 12:15 (NIV) – "Rejoice with those who rejoice; mourn with those who mourn."

Every worship moment carries a different weight.

Some are filled with joy and celebration; others call for stillness and reverence. Not every room, service, or season needs the same response — that's where discernment comes in. Discernment is the spiritual sensitivity to recognize what God is doing now and respond with obedience, not assumption. You might have the perfect set prepared — every transition planned — but if the Spirit leads elsewhere, obedience matters more than sticking to the plan.

Discerning worshippers aren't driven by emotion, atmosphere, or hype. They're grounded in the Spirit and guided by a listening heart. They enter the room asking, "Lord, what are You doing today? What do You want to say?" True worship leadership isn't about executing your vision — it's about stewarding His. It's about hosting His presence and making room for what He wants to do.

This kind of leadership doesn't come from skill alone — it requires humility, spiritual sensitivity, and a consistent prayer life. It means listening to heaven even as you play or sing. It also means laying down your preferences, comfort, and agenda to serve the people in front of you and honour God's movement.

Discerning worship becomes prophetic — releasing God's now word. It becomes pastoral — caring for hearts. And it becomes powerful — because it aligns with heaven, not just human plans.

In worship, timing and tone both matter. Sometimes a whisper carries more weight than a full band. Other times, spontaneous praise breaks through where a scripted set can't.

When you grow in discernment, worship stops being predictable — and starts becoming transformational.

Discussion Questions:

- How can you grow in spiritual discernment as a worship leader?
- Have you ever sensed the atmosphere change during worship? How did you respond?
- What role does prayer play in preparing for sensitive leadership?

Takeaway Activity:

During your next personal worship time, pause and ask God, "What are You doing in this moment?" Then wait quietly and journal what you sense — no agenda, just listening.

25

When Worship Feels Empty

Psalm 42:11 (NIV) – "Why, my soul, are you downcast?... Put your hope in God, for I will yet praise him."

Every worshipper will face dry seasons — moments when it all feels routine, distant, or even empty. You sing, but don't sense God. You show up, but your heart feels far away. These seasons are more common than we admit, and they aren't a sign of failure — they're an invitation to deeper faith. Don't ignore them or fake your way through. Instead, navigate them with honesty, humility, and an open heart.

God is not threatened by your silence, questions, or struggle. He welcomes your vulnerability and invites you to press in, even when it feels hard. These are the moments where real growth happens — not in the ease of celebration, but in the tension of perseverance.

When worship feels hollow, don't retreat — go deeper. Ask yourself: Have I disconnected my heart from my song? Am I leading with faith, or depending on fleeting emotions? David, the ultimate worshipper, wrestled with despair, fear, and silence. But he always circled back to this decision: "Yet will I praise You." That's the power of determined worship.

God values authenticity over artistry. He's not moved by polish or perfection — He's drawn to the honest cry. Your most anointed moments may come when worship costs you something — when it's a sacrifice of praise, not just a celebration of joy.

Keep showing up. Keep lifting your voice, even if it shakes. God sees. God hears. He's still listening — especially in the silence.

Worship becomes most real when it's raw. That's where breakthrough begins.

Discussion Questions:

- Have you experienced a season where worship felt dry or empty? What helped?

- Why does God care more about the heart than the sound?
- What practices can keep your spirit engaged during dry seasons?
- How can worship leaders create space for honest expressions of lament or struggle?

Takeaway Activity:

Write a "Psalm of honesty" — expressing where you're at with God. Include praise, doubt, hope, and longing. Read it aloud as an act of worship.

26

Leading off the Stage

Matthew 6:6 (NIV) – "When you pray, go into your room, close the door..."

Great worship leaders don't just lead from the platform — they lead from their lives.

True influence doesn't begin in the spotlight; it begins in the shadows, in the quiet places where no one's watching. A worship leader's authority doesn't come from their gift or stage presence — it flows from a consistent life of integrity, humility, and surrender. Your public impact will only ever rise to the level of your private character.

How you treat people off-stage speaks louder than any moment on stage. Are you teachable when corrected? Are you kind in conversations that don't benefit you? Do you serve when there's no recognition or reward? These are the questions that shape the soul of a worship leader. Talent may open a door, but character determines what happens when you walk through it.

Jesus gave us the ultimate example of behind-the-scenes leadership. He didn't just perform miracles in public — He withdrew often to pray in private. He didn't just preach to crowds — He knelt to wash feet. He didn't build a platform for Himself — He honored and elevated others. He chose obedience over applause, and humility over hype.

If worship is meant to be a way of life, then leadership must be too. It's not just about what happens during the set — it's about who you are when the service ends. The car ride home. The team debrief. The way you speak to the person on sound, or the new volunteer just learning the ropes. Every moment matters.

Because the kind of worship that truly leads others into God's presence must first come from a life that already lives in it — not occasionally, but consistently. Before your voice ever lifts a song, let your life raise a standard. The most powerful worship leading doesn't start on Sunday — it starts on Monday.

Discussion Questions:

- Why is off-stage character so crucial in worship leadership?
- What does spiritual leadership look like behind the scenes?
- What would change if your ministry was never seen by others?

Takeaway Activity:

Ask yourself honestly: Who am I when no one is looking? Write a personal leadership commitment to live and lead well both on and off the platform.

27

When the Plan Changes

Proverbs 16:9 (NIV) – "In their hearts humans plan their course, but the Lord establishes their steps."

Ministry rarely goes as planned — and that's often an opportunity.

In worship ministry, disruptions are part of the journey. A last-minute song change, a broken guitar string, someone calling in sick, or unexpected leadership shifts — these things can feel like obstacles, but they're also invitations. Invitations to trust, to adapt, and to lean not on our own understanding, but on God's steady presence.

Even the apostle Paul experienced these moments. He had plans, vision, and direction — and still found himself needing to pivot. While we might not always understand why things don't unfold the way we hoped, each detour is a moment to press in, refocus, and remember who's truly in charge. These interruptions aren't always orchestrated by God, but He always meets us in the middle of them.

Flexibility in worship ministry is more than a practical skill — it's a posture of humility. It reflects a heart that says, "God, I trust You even when it's not going the way I expected." When we're more committed to His presence than our plans, we grow. We become leaders who aren't just rehearsed — we're responsive.

Let go of the illusion of control. Prepare well, but hold your plans with open hands. When things shift, choose to see it as a sacred moment to depend on God even more. Allow the tension to produce trust, not frustration. Let it remind you that the goal isn't perfect execution — it's faithful obedience.

You're not called to manage every outcome — you're called to remain available, teachable, and anchored. When you stay flexible, you create space for God to move — in you, through you, and in spite of the unexpected.

Discussion Questions:
- Have you ever had God shift your plans in a worship setting? What happened?
- How do you stay spiritually flexible when things don't go your way?
- Why is surrender essential to worship leadership?
- What's one area you struggle to release control?

Takeaway Activity:

Think of a recent moment where your plans were disrupted. Reflect on what God may have been doing instead. Write a short prayer of surrender for future flexibility.

28

Leading with Vulnerability

2 Corinthians 12:9 (NIV) – "My grace is sufficient for you, for my power is made perfect in weakness."

Real worship begins where the mask comes off.

There's a quiet pressure in ministry to always look strong — to be the one who's got it all together, who's always "on," always full of faith, and never flinching. But worship leadership was never meant to be a performance of perfection. God isn't seeking flawless people; He's looking for faithful ones — leaders who are real, humble, and deeply dependent on Him. Your greatest strength in ministry isn't your polish — it's your posture before God.

Throughout Scripture, we see God consistently using honest, surrendered hearts. David poured out his pain in the Psalms. Elijah battled exhaustion and despair. Paul openly admitted his weaknesses, not to glorify failure but to magnify grace. He didn't hide his humanity — he leaned into it, pointing to God's strength instead of his own. That kind of humility isn't weakness — it's strength under surrender. It's power submitted to a greater purpose.

Vulnerability in worship leadership doesn't mean spilling every detail of your struggle or using the platform as therapy. It means carrying a quiet honesty — a willingness to lead without pretending. It's the courage to say, "I still need Jesus today," and to live in a way that helps others know they're not alone in needing Him, too. It's about being a safe place that points others to the Source of true strength.

When you lead from a place of genuine humility, your worship becomes more than sound — it becomes substance. It becomes real, relatable, and Spirit-led. People aren't drawn to perfection — they're drawn to authenticity. When others sense that your strength flows from God, not from yourself, it builds trust and invites transformation.

Let people see that you don't have it all together — not to lower the bar of holiness or leadership, but to lift their eyes to the One who holds us all together. Because when we take off the mask of self-sufficiency, we make room for God's glory to shine all the more clearly through us.

Discussion Questions:
- What holds worship leaders back from being vulnerable?
- How can sharing your story encourage others?
- What are the risks and rewards of vulnerability in leadership?
- How can you cultivate a team culture of honesty and grace?

Takeaway Activity:

Write a testimony of a time God met you in weakness. Share it with a small group or trusted team member, then pray together.

29

Worship as Surrender

Luke 22:42 (NIV) – "Yet not my will, but yours be done."

Surrender isn't weakness — it's power placed in the right hands. In the garden of Gethsemane, Jesus didn't lose — He gave. His surrender wasn't a retreat; it was the beginning of redemption. When He said, "Not my will, but Yours be done," He set the ultimate example for every worshipper to follow. That quiet, agonizing moment of surrender became the catalyst for our salvation. And now, every worshipper must eventually face the same defining question: Will I hold on to my own will, or will I lay it down before God?

Worship doesn't gain its strength from control — it draws power from submission. It's not about demanding our preferences or insisting on our plans. Worship becomes a spiritual force when it flows from yielded hearts. In God's Kingdom, true authority doesn't come from volume, visibility, or platform — it comes from obedience, from a life that's been fully surrendered to the Father's will.

Surrender is more than a lyric we sing — it's a lifestyle we live. It's not just a moment at the altar; it's a daily posture of the heart. It means releasing the script we wrote for ourselves and trusting the Author who knows the full story. It's loosening our grip on rigid plans, embracing divine detours, and choosing to say "yes" to God — even when that "yes" stretches us, inconveniences us, or costs us deeply. It's the willingness to offer our gifts, our voices, our creativity, our platforms — and ultimately our very lives — for His glory, not our own.

Worship will always, at some point, lead you to the altar. There's no detour around it. And when you arrive there, you bring more than songs — you bring sacrifices. But here's the wonder and mystery of it all: whatever we surrender to God, He never wastes. He redeems it, multiplies it, and uses it far beyond what we could ever imagine.

Discussion Questions:
- What's one area of your life God is asking you to surrender?
- How does surrender deepen your worship?
- Why is surrender often so difficult — even in ministry?
- How can your team model surrendered worship?

Takeaway Activity:

Write a prayer of surrender. Include areas where you've been clinging to control. Offer them to God this week in prayer and practice.

30

The Spiritual Discipline of Rehearsal

Proverbs 21:5 (NIV) – "The plans of the diligent lead to profit..."

Rehearsal is worship — when the heart is right.

It's easy to overlook Monday-night rehearsals or midweek run-throughs as mere logistics, just another task on the to-do list. But in the Kingdom, every moment of preparation carries spiritual weight. Heaven sees the behind-the-scenes. Sometimes the effectiveness of a worship ministry isn't hindered by obvious sin, but by a subtle lack of care, attention, and reverence. Sloppiness in preparation can slowly erode spiritual authority. God isn't only glorified in the spotlight of a Sunday stage — He's deeply honored in the unseen hours, in the tuning, the timing, the teamwork, and the intentional pursuit of excellence.

The Levites didn't wing it. They trained with intention. They practiced with purpose. They were appointed not just because they were musically gifted, but because they understood the sacredness of their service. For them, preparation wasn't just a necessity — it was a form of devotion. Planning doesn't restrict the Holy Spirit — it makes room for Him. A team that is musically and technically prepared can respond with greater freedom. When the practical details are settled, the heart and spirit can engage more fully with what God is doing in the moment.

Let rehearsal be more than coordination — let it become communion. Don't just go through the motions. Pray before you play. Share hearts, not just harmonies. Create a culture where the presence of God is pursued even in the practical. Worship as you warm up. Tune your spirit as you tune your instrument. Rehearsing isn't just about perfecting transitions — it's about preparing a place for God to dwell.

Excellence isn't born on stage; it's cultivated in quiet spaces — in the late nights, the early mornings, the committed midweeks when no one is applauding. When we prepare with passion, purpose, and prayer, we're not just getting ready for a service — we're building a sanctuary. We're setting the table for heaven to meet earth.

Discussion Questions:
- How do you currently approach rehearsal — spiritually and practically?
- What makes rehearsal life-giving instead of draining?
- How can rehearsal become a sacred space for your team?
- What are the dangers of winging worship?

Takeaway Activity:

Before your next team rehearsal, take 5 minutes to pray as a group and dedicate your preparation as an offering to God. Invite His presence into every detail.

31

Partnering with Prophetic Words

Scripture: 1 Timothy 1:18 (NIV) – "Timothy, my son, I am giving you this command in keeping with the prophecies once made about you, so that by recalling them you may fight the battle well."

Prophecies aren't meant to sit quietly on a shelf, collecting dust or waiting for someone else to act on them. They are living invitations—divine blueprints—crafted to stir our spirits, awaken our faith, and call us into intentional action. Each prophetic word carries a seed of promise, rich with potential, and it longs for a willing, obedient heart to respond and partner with God's purposes in the earth. In this booklet, prophetic words from powerful voices such as Smith Wigglesworth, Madeline James, and Roma Waterman speak of a rising sound—a fresh wave of worship, praise, and spiritual awakening—that will emerge from the soil of Australia and ripple out across the nations with lasting impact.

This is not a passive prophecy to be admired from afar. It's a rallying cry for a generation. As songwriters, musicians, and worshippers, we're not bystanders in this unfolding story. We are active participants—co-laborers with the Holy Spirit—called to steward the sound of heaven and amplify it through the gifts and expressions He has placed within us. Songs are far more than melodies and lyrics; they are prophetic vessels that carry the weight and authority of God's promises. They have the power to echo divine truths, give voice to heavenly vision, and become instruments through which breakthrough, healing, and transformation are released.

When we write, sing, and lead with prophetic awareness and spiritual sensitivity, we don't merely create music—we activate movements and release kingdom realities into the atmosphere. We declare what God is doing now, while also preparing the way for what He is about to do. Let's not treat these prophetic words as distant hopes or vague possibilities. Let's pick them up with faith, pray into them with expectation, and release them boldly—believing that the sound rising from Australia will indeed touch the nations, spark revival, and glorify Jesus across the earth.

Discussion Questions:

- What prophetic words have you (or your church) received?
- How can you turn those words into a song or declaration?
- What happens when we align our sound with God's prophetic promises?

Activation:

Choose one prophetic word from the booklet — or one spoken over you personally — and write a chorus or melody inspired by it. Declare it over your life and your nation.

32

Hosting the Presence of God

Scripture: 2 Samuel 6:11 (NKJV) – "The ark of the Lord remained in the house of Obed-Edom the Gittite three months. And the Lord blessed Obed-Edom and all his household."

David, a man after God's own heart, was passionate about restoring the Ark of the Covenant to its rightful place in Jerusalem—a symbol of restoring God's presence among His people. Yet, before the Ark reached the city, it remained in the house of Obed-Edom for three months. During that time, something remarkable happened: the Lord blessed Obed-Edom and all his household. This wasn't a coincidence. The presence of God brought tangible favor, peace, and abundance into his home.

This moment in Scripture reveals something profound: encountering God's presence is not limited to the temple, the tabernacle, or a worship gathering. It's deeply personal. Obed-Edom didn't do anything spectacular—he simply made space for God, and God responded by releasing blessing. Today, as followers of Jesus, we are no longer reliant on an external ark or building to encounter God. We are the temple. According to 1 Corinthians 3:16, the Holy Spirit lives within us. That means we carry the presence of God wherever we go—and we can choose to cultivate that presence in our homes, our families, and our personal lives.

To "host" God's presence is to create space in your life for Him to move, speak, and dwell. It means intentionally aligning your heart, your schedule, and your atmosphere to welcome Him. Worship becomes more than a Sunday activity—it becomes a lifestyle of reverence, invitation, and communion. When we live this way, our homes can become places of peace, healing, and transformation. God's blessing follows His presence.

Obed-Edom's story reminds us that God doesn't just want to visit us on occasion—He desires to abide. His presence brings more than just a feeling; it brings fruit. As you choose to prioritize His nearness, expect your household to be changed. He is a rewarder of those who seek Him. What He did for Obed-Edom, He can do for you.

Discussion Questions:

- What does it mean to "host" God's presence in your daily life?
- How can worship prepare your heart as a dwelling place for Him?
- What are the blessings of prioritizing God's presence in your home and community?

Activation:

Set aside a space in your home where you will intentionally worship and welcome His presence this week. Dedicate time to worship there daily.

33

Worship without Barriers

Scripture: Amos 9:11 (NKJV) – "On that day I will raise up the tabernacle of David, which has fallen down, and repair its damages."

In Amos 9:11, God makes a powerful promise: "On that day I will raise up the tabernacle of David, which has fallen down, and repair its damages." This isn't just a restoration of a physical structure—it's a prophetic picture of the kind of worship God desires. David's tabernacle was radically different from the tabernacle of Moses. While Moses' design emphasized separation—with curtains, courts, and restrictions—David's was marked by openness. There was no veil, no heavy layers of ritual. Instead, worship was central, continuous, and accessible to everyone.

David, understanding the heart of God, established a place where worship and the presence of God were the focus, not religious formality. This foreshadowed the New Covenant reality we now live in, where Jesus has torn the veil (Matthew 27:51) and made direct access to God available to all. We are no longer kept at a distance. Because of Jesus, we can boldly approach God's throne (Hebrews 4:16), not through performance or perfection, but through grace.

This changes everything about how we worship. Worship is not reserved for the spiritually elite or the outwardly polished. It's a wide-open invitation for the broken, the searching, the weary, and the hungry. In our churches and communities, we are called to mirror this open-access model—to create spaces where people don't feel they need to have it all together before they can encounter God.

Sadly, many modern worship expressions can unknowingly rebuild barriers—style preferences, performance mindsets, or unspoken expectations. But God is restoring the spirit of David's tabernacle—a worship culture that is raw, real, and radically inclusive. As worshippers and leaders, we are invited to tear down walls and throw open the doors so that anyone—regardless of their background—can step into God's presence and be transformed.

The restoration of David's tabernacle is not just a prophecy—it's a personal calling. God is raising up worshippers who will carry His heart and host His presence without restriction. Will you be one of them?

Discussion Questions:

- How does the open nature of David's tabernacle reflect what Jesus did for us?
- What barriers keep people from freely encountering God in worship today?
- How can we cultivate a culture of open, welcoming worship in our churches?

Activation:

Pray and ask God to reveal any barriers in your heart that limit your access to His presence. Write them down, then declare His freedom over each one.

34

Gifts in Community

1 Corinthians 12:12 (NIV) — "Just as a body, though one, has many parts, but all its many parts form one body, so it is with Christ."

Spiritual gifts were never meant to function in isolation. God designed His people to operate as one body—interconnected, interdependent, and unified in purpose. Just as the human body relies on every organ, limb, and system to function properly, the Body of Christ thrives when each member plays their part. Every gift, whether visible or hidden, has value. When one part is inactive, neglected, or withheld, the whole body is affected.

On ministry teams—especially worship teams—it's easy to fall into the trap of comparison. We may admire someone else's gift and question the worth of our own. Perhaps you're a background vocalist next to a strong lead, or a tech member serving behind the scenes. But every role matters. God doesn't rank gifts the way people do. He's not impressed by platform or popularity—He responds to faithfulness and obedience.

Comparison is a quiet thief. It steals joy, distorts identity, and can subtly damage team culture. But when we move from comparison to collaboration, something powerful happens. Collaboration fosters unity. It creates a culture where people cheer each other on instead of competing. It opens the door for creativity to thrive, because people feel safe, valued, and encouraged.

Your gift isn't better or worse than someone else's — it's uniquely different. And that difference is intentional. The diversity of the Body isn't a flaw—it's a strength. No one person carries the full picture, but together we reveal more of Christ.

Instead of striving for attention, let's choose to honor one another. Instead of competing for recognition, let's pursue unity. Let's be a team that celebrates together, carries burdens together, and worships God with one heart and many expressions.

Let's move from competition to completion, from insecurity to identity, and from performance to purpose. God placed your gift in the Body for a reason—so bring it boldly, use it with love, and trust that He is glorified when we walk in harmony.

Discussion Questions:
- What do you appreciate about the different gifts represented on your team or in your community?
- How can comparison damage the unity and flow of a team?
- How can you better support or affirm others in their gifting?
- What would a "body" look like if every part tried to do the same thing?

Activation:
Write a note of encouragement to someone on your team who has a different gift than you. Call out the fruit you've seen from their faithfulness.

35

Understanding Our Authority

Luke 10:19 – "Behold, I give you the authority to trample on serpents and scorpions, and over all the power of the enemy, and nothing shall by any means hurt you."

Many believers live unaware of the authority they carry in Christ. Though Jesus has given us power over the enemy and access to heaven's resources, we often walk through life weighed down by fear, doubt, or insecurity. We pray timid prayers, settle for less, and live beneath our spiritual inheritance. But in Christ, we've been given far more than we often realize.

The foundation of walking in authority is understanding our identity. Ephesians 2:6 tells us we are seated with Christ in heavenly places. This isn't just a future hope — it's a present spiritual reality. Being seated with Christ means sharing in His victory, His perspective, and His delegated power. It's a place of rest and divine backing, not striving or self-effort.

Authority in the Kingdom isn't about control or status. It flows from alignment — when our hearts align with God's Word and we are led by His Spirit, our authority becomes active. In that place of surrender and intimacy, we speak with clarity, pray with boldness, and worship with power that shifts atmospheres.

Jesus said in Luke 10:19, "I have given you authority... over all the power of the enemy." That authority isn't earned — it's given. Just like an ambassador represents their nation, we represent Christ. Everywhere we go — our homes, workplaces, and communities — we carry His authority to bring light and freedom.

But to walk in that authority, we must be intentional. We renew our minds with truth, silence lies of powerlessness, and step forward in faith. Authority grows when we use it — in prayer, in worship, in obedience.

You weren't made to live in defeat. You were made to reign with Christ. The question isn't whether you have authority — it's whether you're using it. Will you walk in the fullness of what God has already entrusted to you?

Discussion Questions:
- What does it mean to have spiritual authority as a worshipper?
- How does knowing your identity in Christ affect the way you pray and worship?
- What areas of your life need a greater awareness of God's authority?
- How can you step into your authority with greater boldness?

Activation:

Write a declaration affirming your spiritual authority in Christ. Speak it out loud as an act of faith.

36

Your Testimony

Scripture: Psalm 103:1-2 (NKJV) – "Bless the Lord, O my soul; And all that is within me, bless His holy name! Bless the Lord, O my soul, And forget not all His benefits:

In Psalm 103:2, David says, "Bless the Lord, O my soul, and forget not all His benefits." With these words, he takes an active role in guiding his own heart toward thankfulness and truth. He knows how quickly we can lose sight of what God has done, especially when we're facing pressure, disappointment, or delay. Rather than letting emotions lead, David intentionally reminds himself of God's faithfulness.

Fear and doubt often grow in the soil of forgetfulness. When we lose sight of God's goodness in the past, it becomes harder to trust Him in the present. But something powerful happens when we begin to remember. Gratitude rises. Peace returns. Confidence in God's character strengthens. David lists the benefits — forgiveness, healing, redemption, love, and mercy — as anchors to steady his soul.

There's something deeply faith-building about remembering specific moments where God came through — times when prayers were answered, healing came, or provision arrived just in time. These memories aren't sentimental; they shape our perspective.

They remind us that we're not walking into the unknown alone — we're following the same God who's already proven Himself.

Sharing what God has done not only lifts our own spirits, but it also encourages those around us. Testimonies breathe hope into weary hearts. They proclaim that God is still moving, still healing, still faithful. Every moment of grace we recall becomes a spark that can ignite fresh faith in others.

Take time to reflect. What has God done for you? What prayers has He answered? Write them down. Speak them aloud. Let your history with God shape your response to whatever you're facing now.

You don't need to manufacture boldness — you just need to remember. The God who helped you before is still with you now. And He's not finished yet.

Discussion Questions:

- What are some key moments when you've experienced God's goodness?
- How did remembering past testimonies shift your mindset during a tough season?
- Why do you think the enemy tries to make us forget what God has done?

Activation:

Write a short personal testimony of a time God came through for you. Speak it aloud, declaring it as a reminder of His faithfulness.

37

The Song for the Next Season

Scripture: Isaiah 43:19 (NKJV) – "Behold, I will do a new thing, now it shall spring forth; shall you not know it?"

Isaiah 43:19 declares, "Behold, I will do a new thing, now it shall spring forth; shall you not know it?" God is always moving, always advancing His kingdom. But often, His new work begins quietly—like seeds breaking through the soil. As worshippers, we're called not only to respond to what God has done, but to perceive and prepare for what He's about to do.

Tom Inglis once said, "Every move of God requires a fresh move of worship to accommodate what we've just learned from God." Worship is more than a soundtrack to revival — it's a forerunner. Songs don't just reflect the current season; they help usher in the next one. When we lean in prophetically, we begin to write songs that stir hunger, awaken vision, and prepare hearts for what God is about to release.

This kind of writing requires spiritual sensitivity. It means asking, "What is the Spirit saying to the Church?" and then crafting melodies and lyrics that make space for that reality. You may not have all the language yet — but even a single phrase, hook, or musical idea can carry divine weight and set a tone for what's coming.

God is raising up songwriters who don't just echo what has been but declare what is on the horizon. He's inviting you to see, sense, and sing into the future. When you write from that place, your songs become more than art — they become a prophetic tool for transformation.

Take time to listen. Ask God to show you what's coming — in your church, your city, or your generation. Begin to write, even if it's just a whisper. Trust that He who gives the vision will also breathe on the song.

Discussion Questions:
- What "new thing" do you sense God is doing in your church or region?
- How can your songs help prepare hearts for what's next?
- What does it mean to perceive the times as a worshipper?

Activation:

Ask God to show you a glimpse of what's coming. Write a song or phrase that prepares people for the next move of God — even if you don't fully understand it yet.

www.ingramcontent.com/pod-product-compliance
Lightning Source LLC
Chambersburg PA
CBHW062043290426
44109CB00026B/2711